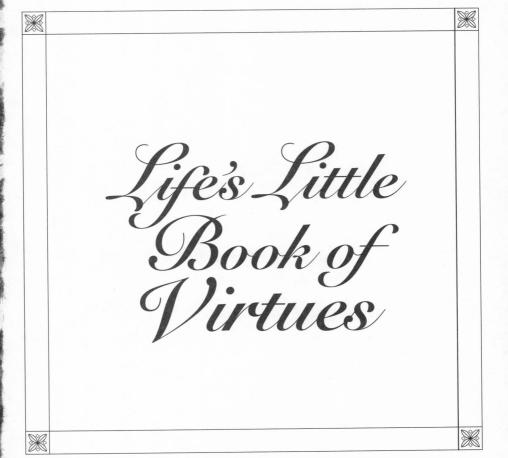

Life's Little Book of Virtues

Life's Little Book of Virtues

JO PETTY

INSPIRATIONAL PRESS

New York

First Inspirational Press edition published in 1996.

INSPIRATIONAL PRESS
A division of Budget Book Service, Inc.
386 Park Avenue South, New York, NY 10016

Inspirational Press is a registered trademark of Budget Book Service, Inc.
Published by arrangement with The C.R. Gibson Company.
Library of Congress Catalog Card Number: 96-77055
ISBN: 0-88486-148-1

Printed in the United States of America.

Foreword

*H*erein are great rules of life

contracted into short sentences that may be

easily impressed on the memory,

and so recur habitually to the mind.

Contents

Love

Life's Little Book of Virtues

Work is love
made visible.

4

To love is virtually to know;
to know is not virtually to love.

Do not judge your friend
until you stand in his place.

Except in occasional emergencies
there is not much that one man can do for another,
other than to help him to help himself.

It is only the forgiving
who are qualified
to receive forgiveness.

A friend is a person with whom you dare
to be yourself.

Love is not soft like water, it is hard like rock,
on which the waves of hatred beat in vain.

Mrs.—Do you love me still?
Mr.—Yes, better than any other way.

We like someone because.
We love someone although.

Always forgive your enemies;
nothing annoys them so much.

A friend is a present you give yourself.

Friends are made by many acts—
and lost by only one.

Politeness is a small price to pay for the
goodwill and affection of others.

It is better to have loved and lost than never
to have loved at all.

Every calling is great
when greatly pursued.

Mothers, as well as fools, sometimes walk
where angels fear to tread.

'Twas her thinking of others
made you think of her.

Some women work so hard
to make good husbands that they never
quite manage to make good wives.

11

Love is the root of all virtues.

The greatest happiness of life is the conviction
that we are loved, loved for ourselves, or rather
loved in spite of ourselves.

If nobody loves you, be sure it is your own fault.

Love understands, and love waits.

Not where I breathe, but where I love, I live.

I hold him great who for love's sake
Can give with earnest, generous will.
But he who takes for love's sweet sake,
I think I hold more generous still.

The remedy for wrongs is to forget them.

Love your enemies, for they tell you your faults.

He who despises, despises not men, but God.

Science has made the world a neighborhood,
but it will take religion to make it a brotherhood.

Increase and abound in love, one toward another,
and toward all men.

We cannot give like God, but surely
we may forgive like Him.

There are shadow friendships that appear
only when the sun shines.

Bless the Lord, O my soul: and all that is
within me, bless His holy name.

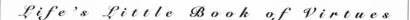

Wear a breastplate of faith and love;
and for a helmet, the hope of salvation.

I shall love the Lord my God with all my heart,
and with all my soul, and with all my mind.
This is the first commandment.
And the second is like, namely this,
I shall love my neighbor as myself.
There are no commandments greater than these.

If I judge not and condemn not,
I shall not be judged nor condemned.

Love never fails.

Love endures all things.

He that spares his rod hates his son:
but he that loves him chastens him.

Love is the greatest thing in the world!

No person is outside the scope of God's love.

Hatred is like an acid. It can do more
damage to the vessel from which it is stored
than to the object on which it is poured.

Love behaves.

Do I love things and use people or love
people and use things?

Love can't be wasted.

A cheerful friend is like a sunny day.

Love hears what the ear cannot.

Love is willing to wait.

Joy

Little and often
fills the purse.

Keep your enthusiasms,
and forget your birthdays—formula for youth!

Money and time are the heaviest burdens of life,
and the unhappiest of all mortals are those who have
more of either than they know how to use.

Joy, temperance and repose
Slam the door on the doctor's nose.

Keep on your toes and you won't
run down at the heels.

Happiness is a perfume you cannot pour on
others without getting a few drops on yourself.

To be without some of the things you want is an
indispensable part of happiness.

The worst bankrupt in the world is the man
who has lost his enthusiasm. Let him lose
everything but enthusiasm and he will come
through again to success.

For all its terrors and tragedies . . . the life of man is
a thing of potential beauty
and dignity . . . To live is good.

What one has, one ought to use; and whatever he
does he should do with all his might.

An unfailing mark of a blockhead is the chip
on his shoulder.

Any person who is always feeling sorry for himself,
should be.

It is not he who has little, but he who
wants more, who is poor.

Old age isn't so bad . . . when you consider
the alternative.

Mirth is from God, and dullness is from
the devil. You can never be too sprightly,
you can never be too good-tempered.

To be happy ourselves is a most effectual
contribution to the happiness of others.

The world belongs to the enthusiast
who keeps cool.

Blessed is the man who digs a well
from which another may draw faith.

Every man's work is a portrait of himself.

One great use of words is to hide our thoughts.

To see God in everything makes life the
greatest adventure there is.

Happiness is the best teacher of good manners;
only the unhappy are churlish.

O, I am grown so free from care
since my heart broke!

Optimist or Pessimist?
Do you call traffic signals go-lights?

Sympathy is never wasted except when you
give it to yourself.

To be wronged is nothing
unless you continue
to remember it.

Visits always give pleasure—if not the coming,
then the going.

Joy is not in things, it is in us.

Almost all men improve on acquaintance.

If you don't make a living, live on what you make.

Life's Little Book of Virtues

Success is getting what you want;
Happiness is wanting what you get.

The deeper that sorrow carves into your being,
the more joy you can contain.

It is when the holiday is over
that we begin to enjoy it.

Pleasures are like poppies spread;
You seize the flower, the bloom is shed.

The best remedy for discontent
is to count our blessings.

It isn't our position but our disposition
that makes us happy.

By reading, I can exchange a dull hour for
a happy hour.

Employ life and you will enjoy life.

Wealth is not his that has it, but his that enjoys it.

I may be poor and have great riches.

To speak kindly will not hurt my tongue.

The place to be happy is here.

Don't just live and let live, but live and help live.

The blue of heaven is larger than the clouds.

It takes both rain and sunshine to make a rainbow.

Peace

In His will is our peace.

If there is righteousness in the heart,
there will be beauty in the character,
If there is beauty in the character,
there will be harmony in the home.
If there is harmony in the home,
there will be order in the nation,
If there is order in the nation,
there will be peace in the world.

In much of my talking, thinking is half-murdered.

Reality may be a rough road,
but escape is a precipice.

The Bible is the book of all others to be read
at all ages and in all conditions of human life.

Pray for others.

Life's Little Book of Virtues

You are none the holier
for being praised,
and none the worse
for being blamed.

Our restlessness is largely due to the fact that we
are as yet wanderers between two worlds.

He does not say,
"at the end of the way you find Me."
He says, "I AM the way:
I AM the road under your feet,
the road that begins just as low
as you happen to be."

Life's Little Book of Virtues

He is only advancing in life whose heart is getting
softer, his blood warmer, his brain
quicker, and his spirit entering into living peace.

He who is taught to live upon little owes
more to his father's wisdom than he who has a
great deal left him does to his father's care.

It's right to be contented with what you have
but never with what you are.

46

Anger is a wind which blows out
the lamp of the mind.

Life is a voyage in which we choose
neither vessel nor weather, but much can
be done in the management of the sails and the
guidance of the helm.

To will what God wills brings peace.

Any housewife, no matter how large her
family, can always get some time to be alone
by doing the dishes.

Fear God and all other fears will disappear.

Pray or be a prey—a prey to fears,
to futilities, to ineffectiveness.

To be content with little is difficult,
to be content with much, impossible.

Be strong and of good courage; be not afraid,
neither be dismayed: for the Lord your God
is with you wherever you go.

Watching for riches consumes the flesh,
and the care thereof drives away sleep.

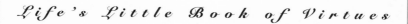

If I am at war with myself,
I can bring little peace
to my fellow man.

If I trust in the Lord and do good, I shall
have a place to live and I shall be fed.

As long as man stands in his own way,
everything seems to be in his way.

The thing to put aside for one's old age
is all thought of retirement.

This is maturity:
To be able to stick with a job until it is finished;
to be able to bear an injustice
without wanting to get even;
to be able to carry money without spending it;
and to do one's duty without being supervised.

Godliness with contentment is great gain.

The peace within becomes the harmony without.

I shall grow old, but never lose life's zest
Because the road's last turn will be the best.
Expect the best!

In solitude we are least alone.

How men treat us will make little difference
when we know we have God's approval.

Life's Little Book of Virtues

Anger rests in the bosom of fools.

Every city or house divided against itself
shall not stand.

As the heavens are higher than the earth, so
are God's ways higher than my ways and God's
thoughts are higher than my thoughts.

Be content
with such things
as you have.

Where envying and strife is,
there is confusion and every evil work.

Better is a handful of quietness than both
hands full with travail and vexation of spirit.

The discretion of a man defers his anger;
and it is his glory to pass over a transgression.

Study to be quiet, do your own business,
and work with your own hands.

Our strength lies in our dependence upon God.

Fret not thyself because of evildoers.

To carry care to bed is to sleep with a
pack on your back.

Long
Suffering

We can do anything we
want if we stick to it long enough.

Patience—in time the grass becomes milk.

Fortune does not change men. It only
unmasks them.

Those who have suffered much are like those
who know many languages; they have learned to
understand all and to be understood by all.

Education should be as gradual as the moonrise,
perceptible not in progress but in result.

Trouble is only opportunity in work clothes.

Life's Little Book of Virtues

A man can fail many times,
but he isn't a failure
until he begins to blame
somebody else.

A man's best fortune or his worst is his wife.

Before you flare up at anyone's faults,
take time to count ten—ten of your own.

The greatest calamity of all is not to have failed;
but to have failed to try.

Education isn't play and it can't be made
to look like play. It is hard, hard work,
but it can be made interesting work.

Fault finders never improve the world;
they only make it seem worse than it really is.

A failure is a man who has blundered
but is not able to cash in on the experience.

Learn from the mistakes of others—you can't
live long enough to make them all yourself.

Great victories come, not through ease but by
fighting valiantly and meeting hardships bravely.

The grinding that would wear away
to nothing a lesser stone, merely
serves to give luster to a diamond.

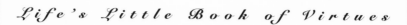

They also serve who only stand and wait.

Sometime, when all life's lessons have been learned,
we shall see how God's plans were right,
and how what seemed reproof was love most true.

Anytime a man takes a stand,
there'll come a time when he'll be tested
to see how firm his feet are planted.

Toil awhile, endure awhile, believe always,
and never turn back.

Fundamentally true ideas possess greater
ultimate power than physical might.

Borrowing trouble from the future
does not deplete the supply.

There are those who are ever learning and never able to come to the knowledge of truth.

Poise is the art of raising the eyebrows instead of the roof.

It is easier to be critical than correct.

Life's Little Book of Virtues

As threshing separates the wheat from the chaff,
so does affliction purify virtue.

Recreation is not being idle; it is
easing the wearied part by change of occupation.

Let me run with patience the race
that is set before me.

The rock of my strength, and my refuge, is in God.

Difficulties
strengthen the mind,
as labor
does the body.

Trying times are times for trying.

The secret of success is hard work.

The dictionary is the only place where success
comes before work.

An ounce of pluck is worth a ton of luck.

Character development
is the true aim
of education.

We first make our habits, and then
our habits make us.

No wise man ever wished to be younger.

A fool utters all his mind; but a wise man
keeps it in till afterwards.

Listening is wanting to hear.

Gentleness

The kindly word that falls today may
bear its fruit tomorrow.

Every noble life leaves the fibre of it
interwoven in the wool of the world.

True nobility comes of the gentle heart.

A gentleman is a gentle man.

Be to his virtues very kind.
Be to his faults a little blind.

Be kind, for everyone you meet
is fighting a hard battle.

We cannot always oblige,
but we can speak obligingly.

A small unkindness
is a great offense.

To listen well is as to talk well
and is as essential to all true conversation.

Man's inhumanity to man makes countless
thousands mourn.

Rejoice with them that do rejoice
and weep with them that weep.

Good manners are
the small coin of virtue.

Life's Little Book of Virtues

A noble heart, like the sun, shows its greatest
countenance in its lowest estate.

It is they who do their duties in everyday and
trivial matters who fulfill them on great occasions.

Culture is one thing and varnish another.

Let not the sun go down on your wrath.

81

To belittle is to be little.

What you dislike in another,
take care to correct in yourself.

A real friend is one who helps us
to think our noblest thoughts, put forth our
best efforts, and to be our best selves.

Withhold not good from them to whom it is due,
when it is in the power of your hand to do it.

If any man desires to be first,
the same shall be last of all, and servant of all.

A reproof means more to a wise man
than a hundred stripes to a fool.

He that hath mercy on the poor, happy is he.

When I think I stand, I should take heed lest I fall.

It were better for me that a millstone were
hanged about my neck, and that I were
drowned in the bottom of the sea, than that
I should offend a little one.

Add to your faith virtue; and to virtue
knowledge; and to knowledge temperance;
and to temperance patience; and to patience
godliness; and to godliness brotherly
kindness; and to brotherly kindness charity.

When you give your alms, do not sound a
trumpet before you, as the hypocrites do . . .
that they may have glory from men.

Let another man praise thee and not thine own mouth;
a stranger and not thine own lips.

When pride comes, then comes shame:
but with the lowly is wisdom.

The meek
shall inherit the earth;
and shall delight themselves
in the abundance of peace.

Goodness

The highest reward for a man's toil
is not what he gets for it, but rather
what he becomes by it.

Praise not only pretends that we are
better than we are; it may help to make
us better than we are.

We've got to build a better man before
we build a better society.

Silver and gold are not the only coin;
virtue also passes all over the world.

To every man there opens a high way and a low
and every man decides the way he shall go.

A man is rich according to what he is,
not according to what he has.

Character is a victory,
not a gift.

The hardest job that people have to do is to move religion from their throats to their muscles.

Though another may have more money, beauty, brains than you; yet when it comes to the rarer spiritual values such as charity, self-sacrifice, honor, nobility of heart, you have an equal chance with everyone to be the most beloved and honored of all people.

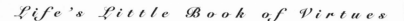

Children need models before they need critics.

What you are in the sight of God,
that you truly are.

Be careful how you live; you may be the
only Bible some people will ever read.

Do right and
leave the results
with God.

I have resolved never to do anything
which I should be afraid to do if it were
the last hour of my life.

Give to him that asks you;
from him that would borrow of you
turn not away.

Can my creed be recognized
in my deed?

Be what you say and say what you are.

Truth cannot be killed with the sword
nor abolished by law.

He that does good for good's sake
seeks neither praise nor reward,
but he is sure of both in the end.

Do good with what you have,
or it will do you no good.

Whatsoever a man sows, that shall he also reap.

If the cake is bad, what good is the frosting?

Legal immunity does not confer moral immunity.

Whosoever shall compel you to go a mile,
go with him two.

A good man leaves a good legacy if he leaves
his children educated.

99

I cannot serve two masters.

It shall be well with the righteous:
for they shall eat the fruit of their doing.

It shall be ill to the wicked:
for the reward of his hands shall be given to him.

To whom much is given,
of him shall be much required.

100

No one has a right to do as he pleases,
except when he pleases to do right.

The eyes of the Lord are in every place
beholding the evil and the good.

If you want to put the world right,
start with yourself.

101

Life is not the wick
or the candle—
it is the burning.

If anyone speaks evil of you, so live
that none will believe it.

There is no right way to do the wrong thing.

The Devil has many tools, but a lie is the
handle that fits them all.

The earth is full of the goodness of the Lord.

We don't break God's laws—
we break ourselves on them.

Conscience is the still small voice that
makes you feel still smaller.

To him that knows to do good,
and does it not, to him it is a sin.

The hand that's dirty with
honest labor is fit to shake
with any neighbor.

Inexperience is what makes a young man do
what an older man says is impossible.

The sectarian thinks that he has the sea ladled
into his private pond.

Anyone can carry his burden, however heavy,
until nightfall; anyone can do his work,
however hard, for one day.

The man who trusts men will make fewer
mistakes than he who distrusts them.

No man is responsible for the rightness of his faith;
but only for the uprightness of it.

The best and most beautiful things
in the world cannot be seen nor touched
but are felt in the heart.

The past
cannot be changed;
the future is still
in your power.

God never closes one door
without opening another.

I'll take the Bible as my guide
until something better comes along.

The body is my house—it is not I.
Triumphant in this faith I live and die.

With God, nothing shall be impossible.

Do the very best you can . . .
And leave the outcome to God.

Fear brings more pain than does the pain it fears.

A man is not old
until regrets take the place of dreams.

Of all the troubles great and small
are those that never happened at all.

If there is no way out, there is a way up.

It is only the fear of God that can deliver us
from the fear of men.

Some folks just don't seem to realize when
they're moaning about not getting prayers
answered, that NO is the answer.

Without the way, there is no going;
Without the truth, there is no knowing;
Without the life, there is no living.

It is not the greatness of my faith that moves
mountains, but my faith in the greatness of God.

When we see the lilies spinning in distress,
Taking thought to manufacture loveliness—
When we see the birds building barns for store,
'Twill be the time for us to worry, not before.

Faith is the substance of things hoped for,
the evidence of things not seen.

Never put a question mark
where God puts a period.

Faith is the victory that overcomes the world.

All unbelief is the belief of a lie.

Use your gifts faithfully,
and they shall be enlarged;
practice what you know, and you shall
attain to higher knowledge.

The horizon
is not the boundary
of the world.

Be persuaded that, what He has promised,
He is able also to perform.

Men do not need to be instructed how to
pray in the midst of battle.

Faith does not exclude work,
but only the merit of work.

By grace are you saved through faith;
and that not of yourselves: it is the gift of God—
not of works lest any man should boast.

The Bible is a surer and safer guide through life
than human reason.

It is impossible that anything so natural,
so necessary, and so universal as death should
ever have been designed as an evil to mankind.

Examine yourselves,
whether you be in the faith;
prove your own selves.

You have not, because you ask not.

A ship is safest in deep water.

Faith
is the eyesight
of the soul.

Train up a child in the way he
should go; and when he is old,
he will not depart from it.

122

If I have faith as a grain of mustard seed,
nothing shall be impossible to me.

The things which are seen are temporal;
but the things which are not seen are eternal.

Ask, and it shall be given to you;
seek and you shall find;
knock, and it shall be opened to you.

Meekness

To know how to grow old is the master
work of wisdom, and one of the most difficult
chapters in the great art of living.

The greatest undeveloped territory in the world
lies under your hat.

If we resist our passions, it is more through
their weakness than our strength.

Never forget that you are a part of the people
who can be fooled some of the time.

There is nothing permanent but change.

Past experience should be a guide post,
not a hitching post.

Life is like a ladder. Every step we take
is either up or down.

A philosopher is someone who always knows
what to do until it happens to them.

Quite often when a man thinks his
mind is getting broader it is only his
conscience stretching.

When success
turns a person's head,
he is facing failure.

Many might have attained wisdom had they
not thought that they had already attained it.

Every man I meet is in some way my superior;
and in that I can learn from him.

It makes a man sort of humble to have
been a kid when everything was the kid's
fault and a parent at a time when everything
is the parent's fault.

The purpose of education is to provide
everyone with the opportunity to learn how
best he may serve the world.

A learned man always has wealth within himself.

Everyone is ignorant—only on different subjects.

They that know God will be humble;
they that know themselves cannot be proud.

An open mind
leaves a chance
for someone to drop
a worthwhile thought
in it.

May I remember that mankind got along very well
before my birth and in all probability
will get along very well after my death.

To accept good advice is but to increase
one's own ability.

Knowledge makes men humble,
and true genius is ever modest.

We may be taught
by every person we meet.

If you have knowledge let others
light their candles by it.

Understanding is a wellspring of life unto
him who has it.

Wealth gotten by vanity shall be diminished;
but he that gathers by labor shall increase.

An admission of error is a sign of strength
rather than a confession of weakness.

God resists the proud,
but gives grace to the humble.

The more you know, the more you know
you don't know.

The ways of man are before the eyes of the
Lord, and he ponders all his goings.

In honor prefer one another.

The greatest truths are the simplest and so
are the greatest men.

Do you care for the poor at your door?

I have wept in the night
for the shortness of sight
That to somebody's need made me blind;
But I never yet have felt a twinge of regret
For being a little too kind.

The test of good manners is being able to put
up pleasantly with bad ones.

True politeness is perfect ease and freedom;
it simply consists in treating others as you
love to be treated yourself.

Few things are more bitter than to feel bitter.

If you are not for yourself, who will be for you?

Listening is a way of loving.

Temperance

Frugality is good if liberality be joined by it.

The driver is safer when the roads are dry;
the roads are safer when the driver is dry.

People who fly into a rage always make
a bad landing.

The archer
who overshoots his mark
does no better than he
who falls short of it.

It is better to keep your mouth shut and be
thought a fool than it is to open it and prove it.

Habit is a cable; we weave a thread of it
everyday, and at last we cannot break it.

In times of crisis we must avoid both ignorant
change and ignorant opposition to change.

We always weaken
what we exaggerate.

If your outgo exceeds your income, then your
upkeep will be your downfall.

Gossip is the art of saying nothing
in a way that leaves nothing unsaid.

Do you spend more than you make on things you
don't need to impress people you don't like?

146

No man is free
who cannot
command himself.

Money may not go as far as it used to, but we
have just as much trouble getting it back.

Sooner throw a pearl at hazard than an idle or
useless word; and do not say a little in many
words, but a great deal in a few.

Habit is either the best of servants
or the worst of masters.

Silence is one of the great arts
of conversation.

Being overly careful about tiny details
of one virtue can't make up for complete
neglect of another duty.

No gain is so certain as that which proceeds
from the economical use of what you already have.

Thrift is a wonderful thing—and who doesn't
wish his ancestors had practiced it more?

Economy is in itself a source of great revenue.

Riches are not an end of life,
but an instrument of life.

Good luck is a lazy man's
estimate of a worker's success.

Willful waste makes woeful want.

Hard work is an accumulation of easy things
you didn't do when you should have.

"The longest way 'round is the shortest way home."
"Make haste slowly." "Haste makes waste."
These are all homely proverbs
with the same meaning; namely,
careful painstaking effort pays in the long run.

Think little
of what others
think of you.

154